◆ LET'S EXPLORE SCIENCE ○

Me and My Body

▲ David Evans and Claudette Williams ☐

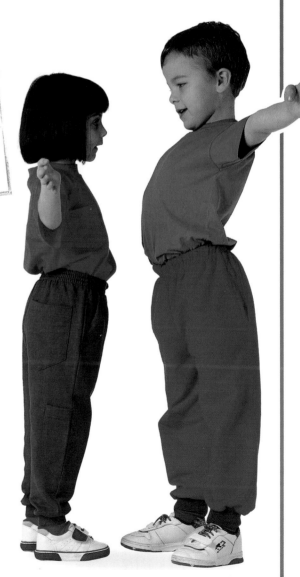

DK

DORLING KINDERSLEY
London ▪ New York ▪ Stuttgart

A DORLING KINDERSLEY BOOK

Project Editor Dawn Sirett
Art Editor Karen Fielding
Managing Editor Jane Yorke
Managing Art Editor Chris Scollen
Production Jayne Wood
Photography by Susanna Price

First published in Great Britain in 1992
by Dorling Kindersley Limited,
9 Henrietta Street, London WC2E 8PS
Reprinted 1993

A CIP catalogue record for this book is
available from the British Library.

ISBN 0-86318-930-X

Reproduced by J. Film Process Singapore Pte., Ltd.
Printed and bound in Belgium by Proost

Dorling Kindersley would like to thank the following for their help
in producing this book: Paul Bricknell and Stephen Oliver (for
additional photography); Coral Mula (for safety symbol artwork);
Gillian Allan; Monica Byles; Mark Richards; Roger Priddy; Chris
Legee; Rowena Alsey; Jane Coney; Julia Fletcher; Jenny Vaughan;
and the Futcher School, Drayton, Portsmouth. Dorling Kindersley
would also like to give special thanks to the following for appearing
in this book: Natalie Agada; Hannah Capleton; Gregory Coleman;
Sapphire Elia; Tyler Henry; Miranda Hutcheon; Tony Locke;
Rachael Malicki; Daniel Moyler; Nathan Moyler; Chloe O'Connor;
Natasha O'Keeffe; Tanya Pham; Maxwell Ralph; Elizabeth Robert;
Jay Sprake; and John Walden.

Contents

Note to parents and teachers

Young children are forever asking questions about the things they see, touch, hear, smell, and taste. The **Let's Explore Science** series aims to foster children's natural curiosity, and encourages them to use their senses to find out about science. Each book features a variety of experiments based on one topic, which draw on a young child's everyday experiences. By investigating familiar activities, such as bouncing a ball, making cakes, or clapping hands, young children will learn that science plays an important part in the world around them.

Investigative approach

Young children can only begin to understand science if they are stimulated to think and to find out for themselves. For these reasons, an open-ended questioning approach is used in the **Let's Explore Science** books and, wherever possible, results of experiments are not shown. Children are encouraged to make their own scientific discoveries, and to interpret them according to their own ideas. This investigative approach to learning makes science exciting and not just about acquiring "facts". It will assist children in many areas of their education.

Using the books

Before starting an experiment, check the text and pictures to ensure that you have assembled any necessary equipment. Allow children to help in this process and to suggest materials to use. Once ready, it is important to let children decide how to carry out the experiment and what the result means to them. You can help by asking questions, such as "What do you think will happen?" or "What did you do?"

Household equipment

All the experiments can be carried out easily at home. In most cases, inexpensive household objects and materials are used.

Guide to experiments

The *Guide to experiments* on pages 28-29 is intended to help parents, teachers, or helpers using this book with children. It gives an outline of the scientific principles underlying the experiments, includes useful tips for carrying out the activities, suggests alternative equipment to use, and additional activities to try.

Safe experimenting

This symbol appears next to experiments where children may require adult supervision or assistance, for example when they are heating things or using sharp tools.

About this book

The experiments in **Me and My Body** encourage children to examine different parts of their bodies and to find out what each part can do. The activities concentrate on parts of the body that are immediately visible, such as skin, facial features, arms, and legs.

Clues are given about the internal workings of the body and the body system. For instance, children are asked to guess where their lungs are.

The experiments challenge children to explore the following:

- the gross structure of the body, i.e., limbs, torso, legs, etc.;
- the senses of touch, sight, hearing, taste, and smell;
- diet (children are introduced to the idea that diet can affect their health).

Children are also asked to compare their bodies to those of their friends or their family. Understanding that humans are all different and that each person is an individual can help children to overcome any anxieties that they may have about their own bodies.

With your help, young children will enjoy exploring the world of science and discover that finding out is fun.

David Evans and Claudette Williams

What are you like?

Do you look like anyone in your family?
Do you look like your friends?

Skin
What is your skin like?

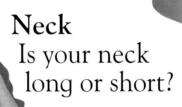

Neck
Is your neck long or short?

Hair
What is your hair like?

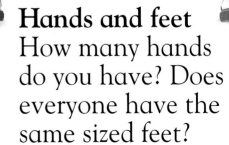

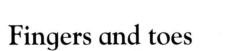

Fingers and toes
How many fingers and toes do you have? Can you make a hand print? What are your fingerprints like? Are your toe prints the same as your fingerprints?

Hands and feet
How many hands do you have? Does everyone have the same sized feet?

Legs
How long are your legs? Can you take a big step? Who can take the biggest step?

Arms
How long are your arms? How wide can you reach? How high can you reach?

Hips, chest, and shoulders
How many hips do you have? Where is your chest? Are your shoulders hard or soft?

11

What can you do?

What do the different parts of your body feel like? What things can you do?

Bones
What do your bones feel like? Are there bones in your feet?

Can you feel and draw the bones in your hands?

Can you feel the bones in a friend's back?

Muscles
Where do you have muscles?

Joints
How do your elbows and knees move? Can you bend and straighten them? Where else does your body bend? How far can you twist round?

Using your tongue
Can you touch your nose with your tongue?

Limbo dancing
Can you limbo under a broom?

Joining fingers
Can you join fingers if you put your hands behind your back like this?

Making a crab
Can you make a crab shape with your body?

13

How big are you?

Find out which of your friends is the biggest.

Are you the same height as any of your friends?

Tall and short
How tall are your friends?

Can you make yourself taller?

Heavy and light
How heavy are
you? How heavy
are your friends?

Push down
hard on some
bathroom scales.
Can you make
yourself heavier?

How heavy
are two of you?

How do you breathe?

Where does the air go when you breathe in? Where does it come out?

Breathing
Take a deep breath in. Then breathe out slowly. Which parts of your body move? Where do you think your lungs are?

Counting breaths
How many times do you breathe in and out in one minute? Can you hold your breath and count to ten?

Moving about
What happens to your breathing when you run, skip, or jump?

Blowing out candles
How many candles can you blow out in one go?

Blowing into water
For how long can you blow down a straw into a glass of water?

Blowing a paper ball
Blow at a paper ball through a straw. How far does the ball move? What will happen if you blow harder?

Blowing up a balloon
How many puffs does it take to blow up a balloon?

What do you feel?

Try these experiments to find out how things feel when you touch them.

Feeling things
Shut your eyes. Ask a friend to pass different things to you.

Can you say what the things are by feeling them with your hands? Do they feel rough or smooth?

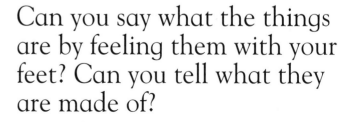

Can you say what the things are by feeling them with your feet? Can you tell what they are made of?

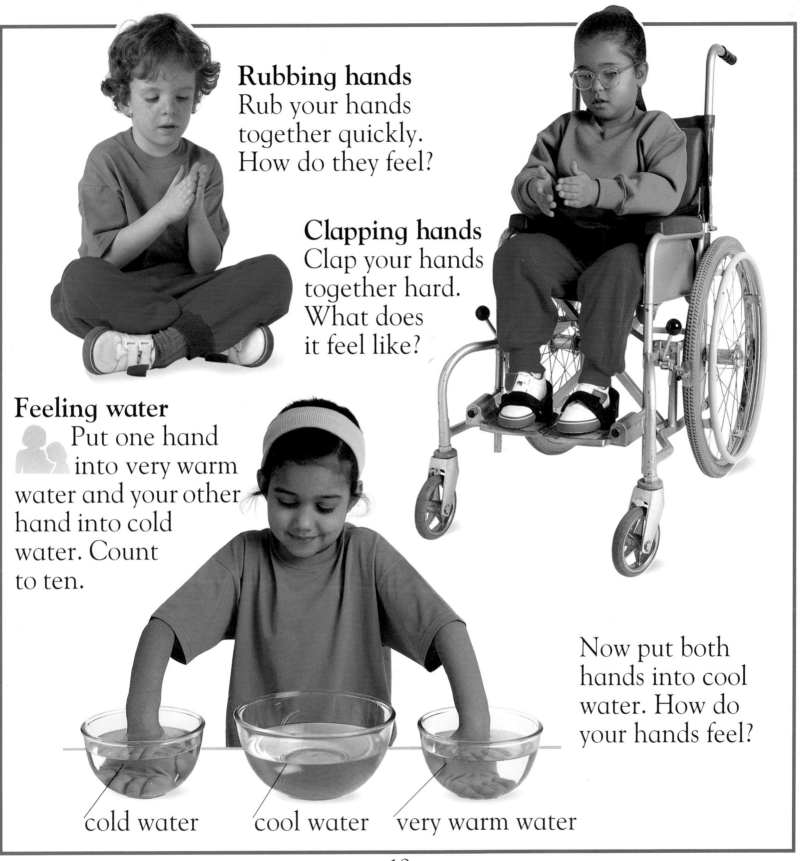

Rubbing hands
Rub your hands together quickly. How do they feel?

Clapping hands
Clap your hands together hard. What does it feel like?

Feeling water
Put one hand into very warm water and your other hand into cold water. Count to ten.

Now put both hands into cool water. How do your hands feel?

cold water   cool water   very warm water

19

What do you see?

Try these experiments to find out about your eyes.

Eyes
Look at your friend's eyes. What do they look like? What is the bit around the middle like?

Look into a mirror. Close your eyes and hold your hands over them. Count to ten. Now open your eyes. Do they change?

Mirror
Can you find your way around a room if you look into a mirror like this?

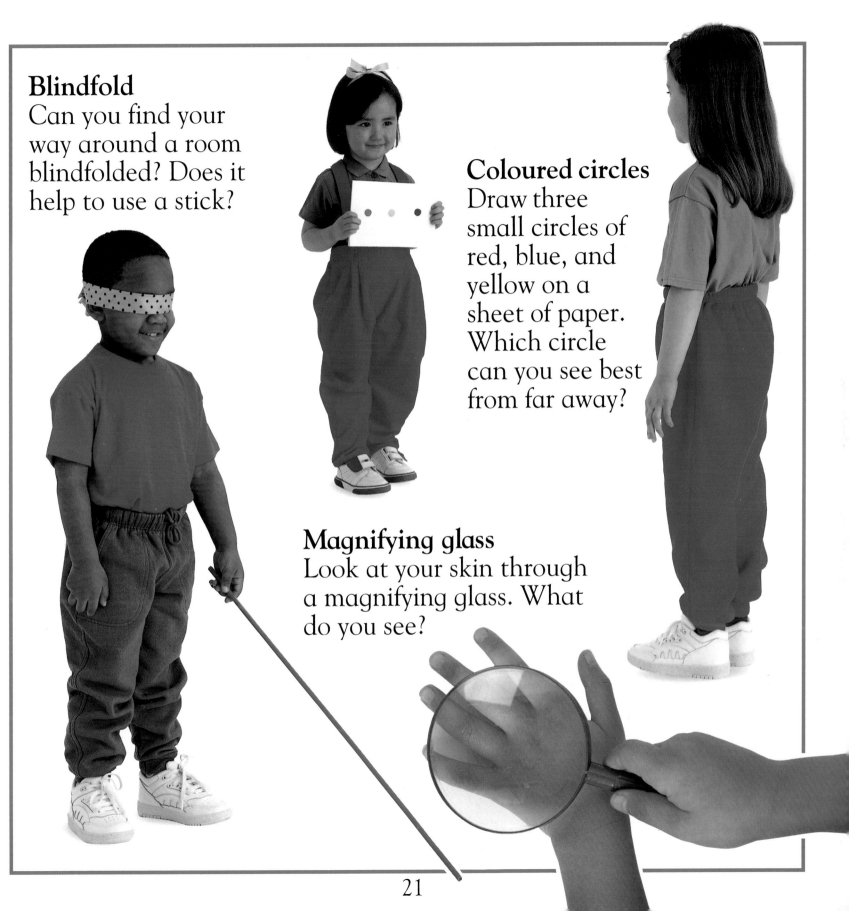

Blindfold
Can you find your way around a room blindfolded? Does it help to use a stick?

Coloured circles
Draw three small circles of red, blue, and yellow on a sheet of paper. Which circle can you see best from far away?

Magnifying glass
Look at your skin through a magnifying glass. What do you see?

21

What do you hear?

Look at your ears in a mirror.
What do they look like?

Looking at ears
Look at a friend's ears. Are
they the same shape as your
ears? What can you see inside
your friend's ears?

Listening to a friend
How far away can you
go and still hear a friend
whispering? What happens
if you cup your hand
around your ear?

Shaking a box
Can you guess what a friend has hidden inside a box if you shake it?

Covering your ears
Cover your ears and walk around a room. Is it easy to walk around if you cannot hear? Try shutting your eyes as well.

Listening to a bell
Ask a friend to ring a bell behind you. Can you point to where the sound is coming from?

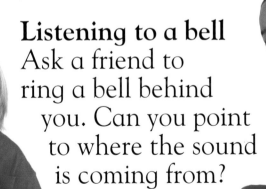

How far away can you go and still hear the bell ringing?

What do you taste and smell?

Try these experiments to find out about your mouth and nose.

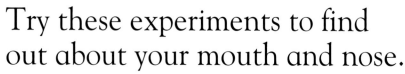

Nose and lips
What is your nose like? What do your lips feel like? What happens to your lips when you say OOO EEE AAA?

Teeth
How many teeth do you have? Are they all the same shape?

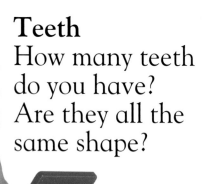

Are your teeth hard or soft?

Mouth
Look into a friend's mouth. Use a torch to help you. What can you see?

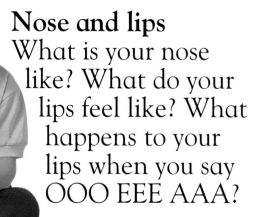
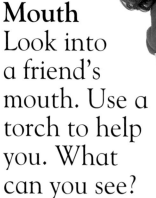

24

Tongue
Is your tongue rough or smooth?
What do these things taste
like when you put them on your
tongue?

salt

lemon

sugar

Tasting
Can you guess what food you
are tasting without seeing it?
What happens if you hold
your nose as well?

Smelling
Which things smell
nice? Which things
have a strong smell?
Do you have a
favourite smell?

25

What do you eat and drink?

What different kinds of food do you eat? What is your favourite meal? What is your favourite drink?

Healthy foods
These foods help you to grow, and stay healthy.

milk

fruit

salad

vegetables

nuts

chicken

eggs and cheese

Do you eat some of these foods every day?
Which of these foods do you like best?

Food diary

Can you draw what you eat in one day? Draw all your meals, drinks, and snacks. Do you eat more healthy foods than snack foods?

bread

Healthy teeth

What would happen if you did not brush your teeth?

pasta

chick peas   lentils   rice

crisps

cake   fizzy drink

sweets

Energy foods

These healthy foods give you energy to run and play. Which ones do you eat most often?

Sweets and snack foods

Too much of these foods can be bad for you and spoil your teeth. Have you eaten any today?

Index

Guide to experiments

The notes below briefly outline the scientific principles underlying the experiments and include suggestions for alternative equipment to use and activities to try.

What are you like? 10-11

Children are given opportunities to look at the similarities and differences between themselves and their family or friends. They can begin to appreciate that despite basic similarities, not all humans are the same. Ask children to name different parts of their bodies.

What can you do? 12-13

These activities enable children to begin to explore what is inside their bodies and what their bodies can do. You can help children to find muscles by asking them if they can see and feel muscles in their legs when they walk on tiptoe. Challenge children to identify things that only they can do, such as wiggling their ears.

How big are you? 14-15

Children learn about size and growth by comparing themselves with their friends. Suggest that they keep a record of their height on each birthday and that they compare hand and feet sizes with their friends.

How do you breathe? 16-17

These activities allow children to explore the way they breathe. As well as asking children how their breathing changes after they have been running, skipping, or jumping, you could suggest that they listen to a friend's heartbeat before and after their friend has been active. When children blow out candles, ask them how far away they can stand and still blow out the candles. Children who are known to be asthmatic should not be encouraged to blow for long periods of time.

What do you feel? 18-19

Here children investigate different sensations and the sense of touch. Another activity children can try is testing the temperature of water with their hands and then their elbows.

What do you see? 20-21

These experiments allow children to explore the sense of sight. Encourage them to talk about the shape, size, and colour of their eyes. Try the mirror activity outside so that children can walk around while looking at the sky. Other activities to try include looking at objects through a telescope or a pair of binoculars.

What do you hear? 22-23

These experiments explore the sense of hearing. Children should look carefully at each other's ears to find differences in shape and size. Good objects to shake in the boxes include corks, marbles, beads, and cotton-wool balls. Another experiment children can try is to distinguish between loud and soft sounds.

What do you taste and smell? 24-25

Here children explore the senses of taste and smell. Another foodstuff to try on the tongue is vinegar. Further experiments include asking children to make lip prints with lipstick and to bite into an apple and examine the imprint of their teeth.

What do you eat and drink? 26-27

Children learn that eating a balanced diet can help them to stay healthy. Ask them which foods they need to eat to keep healthy. Introduce ideas about exercise and personal hygiene, which are also important to health. Ask children how and why they should keep themselves clean.

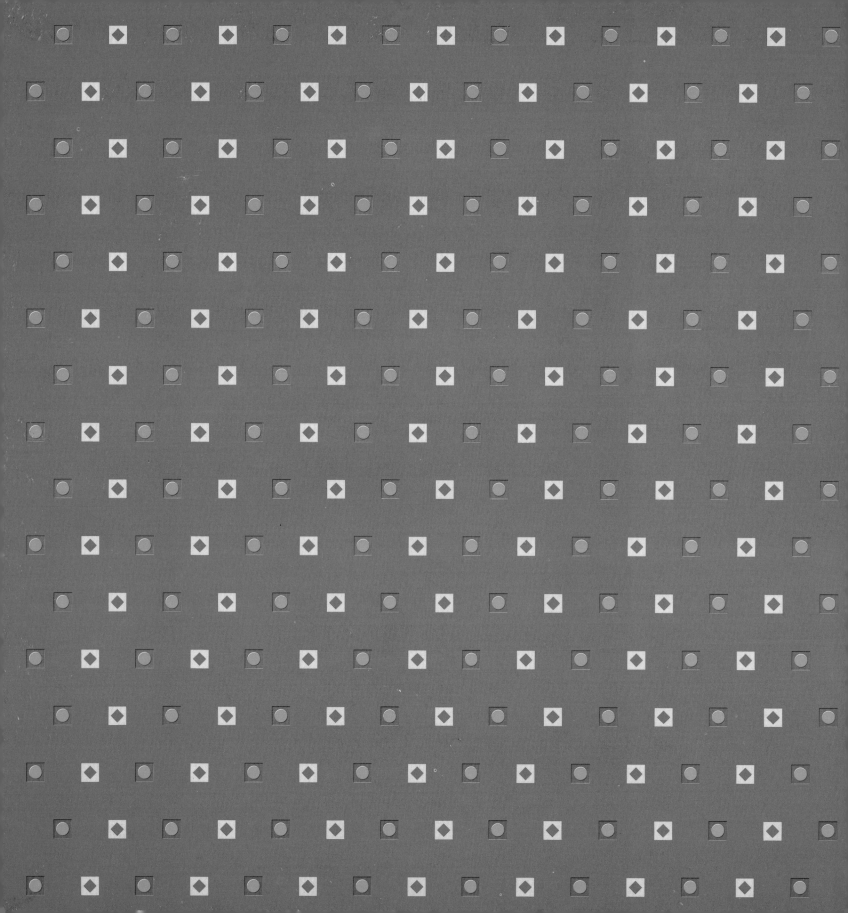